MY RESUME IS PERFECT
IS PERFECT

I think ™

HF
5383
.G37
2009

...SO WHY DIDN'T I
GET AN INTERVIEW?

Fast and easy guide
for students and recent grads
to write a resume
that *gets interviews!*

STACIE GARLIEB

WILLIAM WOODS UNIVERSITY

Copyright © 2009 Stacie Garlieb

All rights reserved. No part of this book may be used or reproduced in any manner whatsoever without written permission except in the case of brief quotations embodied in critical articles or reviews.

ISBN: 1449954618
ISBN-13: 9781449954611

The anecdotes and comments in this book are based on the author's experiences, enhanced by commentary from colleagues. It is not the intent of the author to represent such content as true or to offend or cause malice to any individual or organization. Any resemblance in this book to an actual person, living or dead, is purely coincidental.

ENDORSEMENTS

"In a time when finding a job is tough, Stacie provides the essential tools to prepare the average college graduate for the interview skills he/she will need to impress his/her future boss."

- Jenna Martarano, Community Events Manager, Lucile Packard Foundation for Children's Health.

"This is a comprehensive approach that covers all of the bases in writing a resume which a hiring manager would want to read."

- Larry Shurtz, Vice-President, Fortune 100 Technology Company

"Everybody needs to start someplace when looking for their first professional job, this book is the place to start."

- Doug Blouin, President & CEO Filo Sports Group

. . .

TABLE OF CONTENTS

Introduction 1

My 'Contact Information'
is complete I think 3

My 'Objective' is clear I think 6

My 'Education' information
is crystal clear I think 9

My 'Work Experience' makes me
a good candidate I think 13

My 'Organization and/or Volunteer Experience'
section shows everything I did I think 18

My 'Licenses and Certifications'
are relevant I think 22

My 'Technical/Computer Skills' section
explains my abilities I think 24

My 'Language Skills' section accurately
represents me I think 27

My resume is ready to go I think ...
– Checklist before you send your resume out! 30

'Before' and 'After' Resume Examples 32

Index 43

I think

My resume is perfect **I think**™
...so why didn't I get the interview?©

INTRODUCTION

You had your parents review your resume, your best friend's looks terrible compared to yours, and you got a job at a local restaurant part-time with it, so why aren't you getting interviews with employers that have internship and post-graduation opportunities?

There could be one or more reasons, so this book is intended to help you find ways to make your resume more impactful and user-friendly to a recruiter and hiring manager.

The 'we' in the book is referring to a combined collaboration of recruiters, HR managers, and hiring managers who are currently in positions reviewing resumes from students and recent grads. 'We' know what good looks like, and what bad looks like. Resume review is either the best or worst part of the day for managers, so this book is written to make your resume a positive experience to stand out from the other students!

Take the sections one by one and check out what you are starting with. Be honest about what works and doesn't work for the field you are entering, (we give you some ways to figure out what may and may not work). Don't get emotionally attached to your resume – it's a business document that should be living and breathing and constantly changing as you get more experience in school, organizations, and work. Let it be the initial introduction to an employer that tells them what you can bring to their team.

• • •

My 'Contact Information'

is complete I think ...

Obviously, your name needs to go at the top of your resume (although we have gotten some that have that missing....scary!). If you go by a nickname, now is not the time to tell us that. Let us know that once you have the job offer. One exception, if your name is James and everyone calls you 'Jim', then you can use Jim. We aren't deciding to interview you based on what your name is.

Next is your address, so which should you use, school or home? Best address is the location closest to where the job is – if the job is near school, use that one. If you want to relocate back to Michigan after graduating from a West Coast school, you may want to put your parents' address – this shows that you know the area, which is an added benefit to potentially hiring you. Contacting a company with nationwide jobs? That's a great time to put both addresses if the home and school addresses are both in areas you would like to live post-graduation or for a summer internship. Showing geographic flexibility could add to your chances of getting the interview.

A phone number is next (yes, A phone number, not 2 or 3 numbers....). Number one choice in this case is your cell number (since we know all of you have one) and that way you can control the messages and when you retrieve them. Your roommate might be a great secretary, but the one time an employer calls, something will break on the answering machine or the number will get erased or some other tragedy.

By the way, we don't need your fax number. If we need to fax you, we will let you know and you can give us the number then. That is a 'space filler upper' – information that isn't relevant and just takes up space on the page.

Last, but VERY important is the email address. Ok, so some of you have really creative email addresses, BUT a resume is not the time to have 'chrisrockerdude@aol.com' shared with the world. First name (first initial).last name @ whatever search engine you want to use is the best format. If you can check your spam file regularly, your school address is the best choice – this is where you are spending most of your time, like your job will be, so it is most logical. Some .edu email accounts throw certain extensions into spam though, so when you are actively searching make sure you check that box too.

Here's an example (and there are more in the back – check out the 'Before and After' Resumes)

Tom Maxwell
4444 E. Willow
Phoenix, AZ 85000
(602) 555-1212
thomas.maxwell@gmail.com

• • •

My 'Objective' is clear

 ...

We know that your Objective is 'to get a job' (internship, career opportunity etc) – what we want to know is, "what's in it for ME" the employer to invite you to interview? What skills are the employer looking for that you have? What position are you applying for specifically? Can you get that into one brief sentence – YES!

Here's an example:

Objective: To maximize productivity and revenue as a Territory Sales Representative with XYZ Company by using my communication, organization, and customer service skills.

The key is to keep it short and direct. Employers know why you are sending them a resume, the Objective tells them a few reasons to keep reading and find out more about the skills you listed; where did you get them and what impact did you make with them?

So another way to show what skills make you 'stand out' as a candidate is to put a Summary of Skills section. Don't put both an Objective AND a Summary of Skills. If you do a Summary of Skills, please don't put vague skills like "Excellent oral and written communicator" – tell us a short "where did you get this skill" part. For example – Written communication skills improved through customer interactions at XYZ company OR Customer interaction at XYZ company increased written communication skills. That way we know where on your resume to look down to for more information on what you specifically did at that job.

Be careful of the content in the Summary of Skills though – it should be a 'teaser' to make the recruiter want to read your WHOLE resume. If it looks like 'my opinion of me' without tangible info on where you got the skills, some recruiters may not read any further.

When you aren't sure which way to go, an Objective is always easier to write and accepted as standard by recruiters. As you get more business experience, this turns into a Professional Summary or Executive Summary – you are starting on the right foot to develop it now!

· · ·

My 'Education' information is
crystal clear I think ...

Where you are going/went to school takes primary position – just like where you work will be primary in that section. If you are in a program/college within the bigger institution that would be recognized by a recruiter as famous or important, then list it next. There are a million different descriptions of majors and minors (trust us, we've checked), so it's important to let us know whether you are going to complete a Bachelor of Science, Bachelor of Arts, Associates, or Masters of whatever degree. Minors and Certificates get listed next along with the specialty they are covering.

We know you may be a freshman, sophomore, junior, or senior, so just let us know the month and year you are going to graduate – not necessary to add "Expected to graduate", "Will Graduate" etc – employers do know that if it is 2009 and you put 2011 you are not available for a post-graduate opportunity yet.

Dean's List, or any academic awards, gets their own line if possible! Academic performance is one way to separate yourself from the competition. Did you get a scholarship for GPA and other criteria – put it here. National honors organizations (ones where you get the piece of paper but there isn't any meeting to go to) can be listed here too.

High school information needs to disappear from your resume once you are entering your junior year. At that point, employers are focusing on how you have spent the past two years of school (or more if you have an Associates degree too). A possible exception is high school athletic and organization involvement. Look in the Organization section for more information on this.

So the debate over whether to show your GPA continues....this is a personal decision but we would like to see anything over a 3.0 (or 'B' average) on the resume. If your school measures on a 5.0 scale, make sure you clarify that so we get an accurate picture of your academic performance. Please round your GPA to one decimal point – it's not like 'Pi' (aka: 3.14159....)!

Education:	**New State University**	New Town, AQ	May 2011
	Really Important Person School of Business		
	Bachelor of Science in Business		
	Minor: Business Communication		GPA: 3.2

Dean's List Spring 2009, Fall 2009

National Merit Scholarship 2008
- Awarded to graduating high school students based on SAT scores.

Golden Key National Honor Society Member

Should you include 'Relevant Courses'? Depends on whether the course is unique to your area of specialization (i.e.: Consumer Behavior in US Retailers) that the company – say a large retailer – would be interested in the content. Did you do a semester long project that would be relevant? That could be a bullet point under the course title:

Special Course:
Consumer Behavior in US Retailers   September 2008

◆   Recognized by project review panel of mass merchandiser retail executives
    with highest class grade.

Here's what NOT to do – don't list the core curriculum you have
taken. We actually know that a marketing major has to take some
marketing classes to graduate. Only focus on classes that may be
interesting and special to the company receiving the resume and be
ready to talk about large projects from the class in an interview.

If you studied overseas, here is a great place to make your resume
stand out! Traveling with the parents or friends for a few days doesn't
count. Make sure you include the name of the university program,
dates, location you lived, and what you studied. Showing you can
speak a foreign language can be highlighted here (and repeated in a
separate section later in the book!) too.

Not everyone is going to have all of this – that is what makes each
resume individualized.

International School Overseas   Overseas, Country   Summer 2009

◆   Qualified for two month program for GPA, essay, and interview process.
◆   Learned how to fluently speak Alpha by interacting and living with a Country
    family.
◆   Completed courses in culture, language, art, and business in Country.

• • •

My 'Work Experience' makes me
a good candidate I think …

We know you haven't run a company, or managed a large team of people, or motivated change in an organization yet, you are still in/ just recently out of college. For those of you who have, be sure you take the ideas and include the information about how you did those things. Here are basic guidelines for the rest of us…

First, be sure you include your internships and part-time work experience in this section! Pretty sure that none of you do internships out of your desire for philanthropic work – that's what student organizations are for. Internships – even if you didn't get paid – are work, and employers find great candidates with real-world experience and skills from those positions being included on your resume.

The basic information we want to know is – what company did you work for, where did you do the work (city, state), when did you do the work, what was your title, what responsibilities/activities/projects did you have and what results did you achieve. Don't get stuck on the 'when' part – summer jobs that you do year after year are great – those show employers that someone trusts you enough to have you come back! If it is seasonal work, noting Summers 2008, 2009 is clear to us.

Most important part of each job's information is the 'what responsibilities/activities/projects did you have and what results did you achieve'. Unfortunately, this is also the section most likely to sound like a 'Miss America' answer. Please don't write a paragraph

– most of us are 'old' (over 30) and we need bullet points. Next, a bullet point shouldn't be able to be finished with 'create world peace' or 'solve world hunger' (the Miss America part). If it is too fluffy or lacking the results part go back and make it more real.

Magic formula to make the bullet points 'real' is to add numerical or specific data for the results part. Strong bullet points will have at least 3 of these five criteria:
S pecific
M easurable (how many/much)
A ction-oriented (action verbs)
R esults (numbers or goals met)
T ime bound (over what time period)

So part of this formula is easy because it just takes changing 'soft' verbs to 'action verbs' at the beginning of the bullet point. Check this out:

• Responsible for cash and credit transactions at the register.

Changes to:

• Balanced cash and credit receipts to 100% for register transactions totaling up to $2,000 per day.

Notice that also added in the 'M', and 'R', and 'T'…. It's really not hard, but not every bullet will hit three without some tweaking. The more specific and results oriented your bullets are, the better we can evaluate whether you have skills we are looking for.

And part of making every resume different to meet the needs of what the employer is looking for is to move the bullet points around in order. If I am looking for a Management Candidate, then someone who has 'Collaborated', 'Directed', 'Coordinated', 'Managed', as bullet points in first position under the applicable job is probably going to get a first interview to see if they can really explain their skills in that area.

The next question is 'Which work experience should I include?' – the easy answer is anything you developed or used real-world skills in. Ok, most of you have worked in a restaurant or retail store, right? Bet you have had a difficult customer or a challenging situation with someone ordering/buying something they didn't like. That's problem-solving and probably you were using your communication skills to resolve it. Those are valuable skills no matter where you work or in what industry.

Office work, or work with children or on campus work, all use organization, communication, and time management skills. Think about what you did and what you learned from it. Let's say you didn't learn anything new, but you mastered a skill (think computer programs, organization of an office, using a database or phone system) – that's valuable because then an employer knows that you can learn in the workplace not just at school.

This doesn't mean to over-elaborate on your experience. Be careful of the 'Miss America' factor – if we think you "made up" one thing, we may think other parts are made up too. Make sure you are truthful and accurate so when you get to the interview you can use those bullet points to develop stories about what skills you bring to the table.

Here are some of examples of work experience sections:

ABC Coffee Company   Town, State   Summers 2005, 2006
Coffee Maker
- Collaborated with team of 4 employees for 8 hour shift achieving store revenue goal of $3K daily.
- Exceeded daily sales goals by 55% per management direction with over 250 customer interactions.
- Managed opening and closing store including all daily finance and inventory activities at highest volume New State store.
- Learned how to effectively use visual merchandising to maximize revenue in 3 window and 5 in-store displays.

Non-Profit Company   People Town, Old State   September 2007 – Present
Intern
- Assist in creation of nine promotional pieces for fundraising events resulting in 1000 people attending.
- Research fifty marketing contacts for support and contact them weekly via email and phone.
- Coordinated silent auction items for display with 100% purchase at event end.
- Maximized donations from businesses through a database and follow up increasing future support.

John's Cosmetic Store   All Towns, New State   June 2004 - Present
Sales Representative   Back Home, Parents' State Summers 2002, 2003
- Develop client relationships for 200 customers daily by having strong product knowledge and customer service.
- Consult with clients on benefits of products in nineteen cosmetic lines to meet their needs
- Created displays promoting more than 1500 full price and sale items with 106% increase in summer sales.
- Assist two managers with inventory management monthly including floor sets and mannequin placement.

And you don't need to have 'four' bullet points per job either — these are just examples. A job that only has one bullet point will look weak though, so think about what you did or learned and be specific about it. Make sure your bullet points make sense, so if you did it in the past, please use past tense, and if you are doing it still in that job, make it present tense. We know you are all experts at the computer, so please use 'Tools – Spelling and Grammar' (or the Mac or PDF equivalent) before you send us a resume!

My 'Organization and/or Volunteer Experience' section shows everything I did I think ...

In this section you want to include any student organizations in school (remember, no high school after sophomore year) that you participate in. If you are a student athlete, then you could include high school if there was a significant event – state/regional/national awards or finals – but try to focus on the collegiate experience after sophomore year.

So, let's say you are in a club that only meets once a month and is a way to meet other students in your major. You have to make the call on that one, and we would say if you use it to network and meet employers or increase your professional development skills then it's valuable.

What if the club is for recreation and you are passionate about that (Surfing Club, Rock Climbing Club, Historical Fiction Reading Club etc)? Then I would decide when to include that based on the job – did you find out the person you are sending the resume to lists surfing as an interest on their Facebook® or LinkedIn® profile – put it in. Maybe the job is working for Dan Brown's publishing house – the Historical Fiction Reading Club would be important. Watch who your audience is for the resume and then choose. If you don't know the person and can't make the call, leave it off unless you have/had a leadership position that shows skills you got from being involved.

Obvious clubs to include are ones that help you network, develop skills for your specialty (accountancy club), or Greek Life. Whether your audience was personally involved in those types of clubs doesn't matter, it's how you explain (with bullet points) what you got out of it that makes an impact to an employer. If you make it sound like you partied like a rock star then you will have an issue.

Not everyone is on 'council, executive board, committee chair' and that is ok. If you are/have been, make sure you show bullet points with your responsibilities – how many people 'reported' to you, did you manage a budget, were there reports that you submitted to the school or national organization, what improvements/developments in the organization (think number of members, changing events, increasing school presence) did you work on and execute.

The bullet points need to be SMART – go back to the 'Work Experience' section if you forgot – and meaningful/not obvious. If you are President we actually know that you 'Led a chapter for annual events'. Create those bullet points to scream out to the employer the specifics of what we won't automatically know about your organization.

If you were an active member, then include a bullet point (or more if applicable) about what programs/projects/events you participated to support the organization. Did you help with recruitment (every club recruits otherwise you would not be on campus year after year), what about philanthropies/charity events, was there an intramural/sports/academic competition that you participated in representing the club?

Here are some examples:

National Social Sorority   Town, State   January 2003 – Present
Vice-President of Membership   November 2004 – November 2005
- Developed and managed action plan and budget of $10,000 for recruitment of 80 members in Spring.
- Exceeded recruitment goals by 20% for national organization based on quota for ABC Greek system.
- Created team activities to execute local goals and motivate retention of members.

Philanthropy Chairperson
- Designed plans for 150 members' activities raising $5,000 in funds to support national philanthropy.
- Negotiated pricing with twenty vendors for tournament locations, prize donations, and catering.

Business School Organization   Old Town, New State   Fall 2008 – Present
Networking Committee   Spring 2008
- Developing concept, agenda, venue, content, and timeline for execution for annual dinner for 30 members.
- Coach and teach ten new members on various topics for interacting with guest speakers and potential employers weekly.

Senior Support Club   Town, State   Fall 2006 – Fall 2008
- Volunteer for local shelter with 75 club members to teach crafts and arts to more than eighty seniors.

Big Siblings Organization   New Town, State   July 2009 - Present
- Selected to mentor high school student for one year, after interview process with eighteen other candidates.
- Coordinate bi-weekly activities including extracurricular events resulting in improved self-esteem for the individual.

My 'Licenses and Certifications' are relevant I think ...

This section really only applies to a certain percentage of you. If you are in education and have received certificates for special education areas (language, special needs etc), then you can list those certificates here. They also could go into the Education section so you choose what makes more sense — if you are applying for a job specifically in that field, we would rather see it up higher in the resume. Same situation with specialized technical certificates for engineering, architecture, CIS, etc.

Some of you may have gotten a license that may not apply to the job you are applying for — please don't include it. When someone with a real estate license is trying to get into a development or construction oriented company it may make sense to include that information because they learned something about the industry. This is definitely too much information (TMI) for a resume being submitted for a corporate management training program outside that field.

Certificates and Specialized Training:

Reading Specialist Certification K-12th	Valley, State	January 2007
Early Childhood Endorsement	Valley, State	May 2006
Special Language Certified	Valley, State	August 2005

Professional Licensure

State Reading License	Old Town, State	Expires May 2015

My 'Technical/Computer Skills' section
explains my abilities I think ...

We know you can use a computer to create a resume, but what programs you can use and on what types of computers is important. Since we personally know some 'old' (over 40) people who can't figure out Word, we want to reinforce the great technical benefits you can offer an employer! So make sure to include if you can 'Mac' and 'PC' – we are really impressed if you do both because most of us can't (or won't...).

Being able to take 'red eye' out of your friends pics in Photoshop doesn't make it relevant to the job – unless it's a photography one- so think about that before you include it for certain employers. Graphic arts/design/architecture candidates need to list ALL relevant programs for the job. Ditto for CIS, engineering, or other technical fields. Evaluate what you include based on the job description and the company.

What if you learned how to 'manage a database' at a job – include this in the job under work experience. How about SPSS for marketing majors, well that depends on whether you would use it at that company. And those of you who are in journalism and broadcasting have another whole set of programs to make sure and include. Social media networking (Facebook® and LinkedIn® and blogging etc.) could also be important to include depending on the position. Bottom line is if you would use those skills/programs at the job, include them!

Computer Skills: Microsoft Word, Microsoft Excel, Microsoft PowerPoint, SPSS, Adobe Acrobat

COMPUTER SKILLS Microsoft Office Suite and Macintosh Pages, Numbers, and Notes, Blog software

Technological Skills: Microsoft Word, Excel, PowerPoint, Macintosh Pages, Dreamweaver, Adobe Illustrator

My 'Language Skills' section accurately represents me I think ...

Just remember that not everyone will have this section. Some of you took high school language and haven't used it since Mom said you didn't have to take another year of it to graduate. Others of you took a language that seemed really cool but you would have to move or travel overseas to use it (and that's ok and may count depending on the job/company you are applying for!).

Whether the job specifically lists 'Spanish language skills preferred' or not, there are some languages that we recommend would be included on every resume:
Spanish, Asian languages, Arabic, Italian and Portuguese (similar in structure to Spanish), American Sign Language

What if you lived in Germany for overseas study and you might be able to hold a conversation, but probably not a very long one? Best not to include that, because would it really help an employer in the workplace? Why not include your French language skills if you took it in high school and college – if it's relevant to the geography or job or industry, then put it on. Same deal with Latin, Greek, and pretty much any other language we didn't already list.

Grandma always spoke to you in Dutch and you understand it fluently and converse, read, and write it. Then you have to make the call if this would be a benefit to show your ability to be multi-cultural – we would say yes, but be prepared. If you have a Dutch interviewer and you can't carry on a conversation if asked to, that would be a disaster!

Language Skills Conversationally proficient in Spanish

LANGUAGE SKILLS: Fluent in Mandarin Chinese
Conversationally fluent in Russian

My resume is ready to go **I think** ...

Here's a final Top 10 checklist to help you make sure you have a resume that will get a recruiter's attention:

- ✓ Font size no smaller than 10pt and margins no smaller than .4 all around
    - ○ Your margins should be as close as possible on top to bottom and left to right. It looks really bad to have a 1" margin on the left and .5" on the right!

- ✓ First page has the MOST important information – they may not get to the second page!
- ✓ No excessive lines (underlining some content is ok), no bubbles – yes, we have received resumes with bubbles - no pictures of yourself (unless you are applying internationally), no graphics (unless you are in the arts or design etc.).
    - ○ Some companies use software like colleges do for plagiarism to 'screen out' resumes – some of that software will dump resumes with lines separating sections or across the top or down the side into the 'trash file' in their system before anyone actually could get a chance to read it.
    - ○ Resumes are NOT supposed to be 'works of art' – it's a business document. We are not evaluating 'pretty, prettier, prettiest' resume to decide who to call for an interview!

- ✓ Contact information is complete and appropriate for a business document
- ✓ Clear Objective specific to the company and position OR Summary of Skills with specifics on where you got the skills
- ✓ Education information has all my awards, degree information, and graduation date listed
- ✓ Work experience includes all relevant work including internships

  - o Bullet points under the jobs, NOT paragraphs
  - o Reverse chronological order - most recent at the top, to least recent
  - o Meaningful RESULTS in the bullet points – no Miss America bullets
  - o Don't use "I" in the bullet points, or anywhere else on your resume, it's your resume so we know YOU did it

- ✓ Organizations and/or volunteer work is detailed with accomplishments and positions held
- ✓ Computer and special technical skills are listed – don't forget to list PC AND Mac
- ✓ Language skills are listed with a definition of your level of ability

One last note:
Don't put 'References Available', 'References upon Request', or anything about references on your resume

  - o If we want to hire you, we will ask you to fill out an application and then you will need to give us references for a background check
  - o Putting this on your resume just takes up space you could use for information we want to know!

Now you can check out a few examples of 'Before' and 'After' resumes....

I think

Ellen Cryter

555 E. Broadway Rd
New Town, State 80000

(555) 555 - 1212
elhotchick@
hotmail.com

Objective

To gain experience in the business industry through performing an internship.

Education

2007 - Present A State University, New Town, State
Junior – Business and Mass Communications major
- G.P.A 3.00
- Completed 72 units

Employment History

Retail Sales Associate

Fall 2007 – Spring 2008 GUESS What?, INC. New Town, State
- Gained and developed ability to accommodate customers in diverse situations
- Developed strong customer service skills performing numerous transactions.
- Communicated with and assisted customers, staff, and management
- Top sales associate, breaking multiple sales records.

Assistant Office Secretary

Fall 2006 – Winter 2007 My High School, New Town, State
- Aided in daily accommodations for customers to the pro shop.
- Communicated daily with management, staff, and members

Secretarial and Financial Assistant

Fall 2004 – Winter 2006 Family Company, New Town, State
- Assisted in daily secretarial needs, such as word processing and customer service.
- Assisted with payroll, billing, and bidding processes.

Tutor for struggling and troubled children

Fall 2002 – Summer 2003 New Town, State
- Worked with hard-to-handle third and fourth graders
- Taught and strengthened their skills to read and write bringing them up to the level of their classmates.

Other Experience

Current member of Alpha Beta Delta sorority
Speak and understand Spanish
Mac and PC user

Ellen Cryter

555 E. Broadway Road
New Town, State 80000
(555) 555-1212
Ellen.cryter@su.edu

Objective: To utilize my communication, interpersonal, and educational skills to secure an internship position with a dynamic real estate development organization.

Educational Experience:

A State University	New Town, State	December 2011
Bachelor of Science in Business and Mass Communications		GPA: 3.0

Work Experience:

Guess What? Inc.   New Town, State   November 2007 – May 2008
Retail Sales Associate
- Exceeded sales goals monthly by 120% for eight consecutive months.
- Awarded Top Sales Associate every month while exceeding higher sales goals each month.
- Increased product knowledge on 150 items through training with various levels of management team.
- Provided exceptional customer service resulting in return customer rates exceeding 95%.
- Opened and closed store including balancing register to 100%, security checks, and merchandising of displays prior to close.

Family Company   New Town, State   November 2006 – November 2007
Office and Financial Assistant
- Processed payroll, account billing, and customer bids which increased profitability by 25% annually.
- Managed confidential financial transactions and client database for 15 employees monthly.
- Created positive environment for over fifty new and existing customers through elevated customer service and attention to detail.

My High School   New Town, State   August 2006 – January 2007
Assistant Office Secretary
- Coordinated administrative tasks including filing and phone reception at school with 450 students.
- Interacted with 80 teachers, students, and office staff at weekly meetings and for individual needs.

Organizational Experience:

Alpha Beta Delta National Sorority   New Town, State   August 2007 - Present
Personal Development Chair   November 2008 - Present
- Organized monthly speakers for chapter meetings on topics including personal safety, etiquette, and professionalism while managing a budget of $2,000.
- Collaborated with eighteen Greek organizations for philanthropic events generating over $25,000 in funds for national Alpha Beta Delta charities.
- Recruited 40 new members per semester which resulted in exceeding quota goals each semester.

Language Skills: Conversationally proficient in Spanish

Computer Skills: Microsoft Word, Microsoft Excel and Microsoft Power Point
Macintosh Pages, Macintosh Numbers, and Macintosh Notes

Mark Alexander

555 W. Main Street
New Town, State 90000
(555) 555-1212
Malexander5183@gmail.com

OBJECTIVE   To obtain employment with a retail store.

TRAITS/ SKILLS

- Positive team player
- Excellent verbal and written communication
- Hard-working and motivated individual
- Responsible and reliable with any task I am given

EDUCATION
8/05- 5/09

University of State   New Town, State
G.P.A. 3.83, Magna cum Laude
Major: Journalism
Minor: Portuguese
Portugal Exchange University   Foreign Town, Portugal
- Took classes and attended art, music, and religious events

Computer skills with Microsoft Office. Macintosh, and Dreamweaver programs

WORK EXPERIENCE
Spring 2008

Mark's Shoe Store   New Town, State
Salesperson of customized shoes
- Interacted with customers to assess their needs in footwear
- Used product knowledge to effectively sell products customers liked

Summer 2007

New Expensive Store at the Mall   New Town, State
Salesperson in the Really Expensive Shirts department
- Applied skills in customer service
- Trained to use register

Summer 04, 05, 06

Carson's Medical Equipment Inc.   New Town, State
Billing Assistant
- Developed understanding of how to respond to the requests of management
- Learned time management skills

Fall 2003

Point of No Return Sports Center   New Town, State
Desk Person
- Used and further developed communication skills in working with clients
- Learned to be responsible and reliable in managing monthly dues of clients

ORGANIZATIONS
8/07- Present   **Gamma Alpha Theta**
8/06- Present   **Lambda Pi Alpha Journalism Honor Society**
8/06- Present   **Golden Key International Honor Society**
12/06-Present   **Sigma Lambda Omega National Leadership and Honors Organization**
1/07-5/09   **American Marketing Association**
3/07-Present   **Phi Beta Kappa Honor Society**

AWARDS AND HONORS
Spring/Fall 06/Spring 07   **Dean's List Honorable Mention**
Spring 08   **Dean's List**

REFERENCES   *Available upon request*

Mark Alexander
555 W. Main Street
New Town, State 90000
(555) 555-1212   malexander@gmail.com

OBJECTIVE

To obtain a part-time position utilizing my communication, interpersonal, and organization skills within a specialty retail store, resulting in increased revenue.

EDUCATION

May 2009

University of State   New Town, State
Major: Journalism
Minor: Portuguese   Magna cum Laude Honors (3.8 GPA)
Dean's List Spring and Fall 2006, Spring 2007, Fall 2008

May 2008- August 2008

Portugal Exchange University   Foreign Town, Portugal
- Collaborated with international students on presentations and research.
- Gained knowledge and sensitivity of cross-cultural lifestyle practices.
- Successfully completed language, athletics, and history classes.

December 2006 - Present   **Sigma Alpha Lambda National Leadership and Honors Organization**

August 2006 - Present   **Lambda Pi Eta Communications Honor Society**

August 2006 – Present   **Golden Key International Honor Society**

March 2007 - Present   **Phi Beta Kappa Honor Society**

WORK EXPERIENCE

January 2008 – May 2008

Mark's Shoe Store   New Town, State
Salesperson
- Developed relationships with more than 200 clients monthly.
- Consulted with management on new concepts for merchandising and sales which led to 20% increase in sales monthly.
- Assisted with inventory management reducing returns and damages 30%.
- Created window displays promoting sale items and increasing retail sales.

June 2007 – August 2007

New Expensive Store at the Mall   New Town, State
Salesperson
- Chosen for Really Expensive Shirt section helping over 50 clients weekly.
- Trained on Sales and Customer Service processes over a two week period.
- Accurately managed monetary transactions with 100% balances at shift end.

Summers
2004, 2005, 2006

Carson's Medical Equipment Inc.   New Town, State
Billing Assistant
- Organized confidential client information including billing through forty managed care companies such as Medicare.
- Constructed sales training materials with information from ten vendors.
- Completed office reorganization including filing and phone system change.

August 2003 – March 2004

Point of No Return Sports Center   New Town, State
Desk Assistant
- Communicated with 250 clients weekly on membership and game questions.
- Managed monthly dues of clients securing 90% on time payment.

ORGANIZATIONAL EXPERIENCE

August 2007 - Present   **Gamma Alpha Theta National Fraternity**   New Town, State

January 2007 – May 2009   **American Marketing Association**   New Town, State

TECHNOLOGICAL SKILLS   Microsoft Office Suite, Macintosh Pages and Notes, Dreamweaver

Alison Jackson

555 N. Wilson Road
New Town, State 20000
(555) 555 - 1212

KEY OBJECTIVE
A driven individual seeking full time employment within a organization in order to utilize my skills and promote company growth.

EDUCATION
A State University   **Expected Graduation: May 2011**
Famous Person School of Communication
Bachelor of Science: Communication
Minor: Marketing
A Bachelor of Science in Communication with a sub-concentration in Marketing.

EXPERIENCE
Specialty Retailer – Department Manager   **Jan. 09 – Present**
Build solid relationships with all clients. I coordinate with different companies that help us with buying and promoting products while I communicate with our PR firm.

Healthcare Company Services – HR Assistant   **Aug. 08 – Dec. 08**
Build and maintain relationships with clients and employees. I organized events for all of the employees and clients to better familiarize them with the company and increase sales. Management asked me to create a new marketing campaign for customers.

Cable TV Show Pilot – Promotions Person   **April 07 – May 07**
Developed ideas that would help promote a reality television show. This position gave me the ability to work hand in hand with the auditioning crew of the show. Used the Visio Database system.

Local Film Festival – Foreign Country– Intern   **May 07 – June 07**
This internship provided me with knowledge of the film industry. I worked directly with producers, directors, and actors. Experiencing this helped me to know about language in the entertainment industry.

ACTIVITIES AND AWARDS
Chi Beta – A State University   **Aug. 08 – Present**
Chi Beta is committed to community service, support of the Greek Life organizations on A State University's campus, and national support of our philanthropies.

Offices held:
- **Pledge President** – Organized all the events, education, and chapter schedule programs for the Pledges.
- **Vice President for Membership** – Created events, senior week, and house retreat that everyone attended.
- **Recruitment Person** – Maintained a group of girls and helped them through the process of recruitment

Alison Jackson
555 N. Wilson Road
New Town, State 20000
(555) 555-1212
alison.jackson@aol.com

OBJECTIVE
To utilize my creativity, customer relationship development, and communication skills to increase efficiency as a Production Assistant in the Alphabet Networks organization.

EDUCATION
A State University   Old Town, State   May 2011
Famous Person School of Communication
Bachelor of Science in Communication   Minor: Marketing

WORK EXPERIENCE
Specialty Retailer   Old Town, State   January 2009 – Present
Department Manager
- Develop partnerships with clients such as Old Town Magazine, Blue Horse, and Adam Trellis fashions, resulting in a 30% increase in revenue.
- Coordinate media relations activities around advertising in magazines by creating visuals.
- Collaborate with six salespeople on quarterly objectives via verbal and written communication.

Healthcare Company Services   Old Town, State   August 2008 – December 2008
HR Assistant
- Built and maintained relationships with over 30 clients and 25 employees through consistent communication of company directives and goal attainment.
- Organized four client appreciation events for employees to network with new and existing clients.

Cable TV Show Pilot   Parents' Town, State   April 2007 – May 2007
Promotions Person
- Surveyed community members on content, name, and creative logo for a local cable pilot.
- Assisted with pre-production details such as casting, wardrobe, set design, and prop purchases.

Local Film Festival   Foreign City, Country   May 2007 – June 2007
Intern
- Communicated agendas and timelines with 15 producers, directors, and actors from the US.
- Created timeline and coordinated transportation for talent to travel to and from Film Festival.

ORGANIZATIONAL EXPERIENCE
Chi Beta Sorority   Old Town, State   August 2008 – Present
Vice President of Membership Development   November 2009 – November 2010
- Developed and executed events (Senior Week and House Retreat) for 110 members including contracting with the hotel, selecting menu items, and planning the agenda.
Recruitment Counselor   August 2009 – September 2009
- Managed and supported 30 new A State students through the process of recruitment with 95% attaining membership into national sororities.
Pledge Class President
- Organized education classes and three sisterhood events for 20 new members with 100% achieving goals and being initiated.

COMPUTER SKILLS
Microsoft Word, Excel, and PowerPoint, Visio Database System, Adobe Acrobat

ANDREW JOHN FRANKIN
Afrankin@email.university.edu

Current Address	Permanent Address
555 North Central Avenue Apt. #2 New Town, State 80000 (602) 525-5430-Cell	111 South 4th Street Old Town, Other State 50000 (480) 991-7895 Home Phone

EDUCATION: **University of State**   New Town, State
Bachelor of Science, expected December 2012 graduation
Major: Engineering
Minor: Computer Sciences

EXPERIENCE:

5/09-7/09   **Anderson Engineering Firm**   Old Town, Other State
Internship
-Handled phone calls with clients and informed them of future projects the company was developing in different areas of town.
-Made spread sheets on Excel to detail the company projects and progress
-Met with management about what projects were going to move forward

5/08-7/08   **Hometown Restaurant**   New Town, State
Server
-Showed great customer service skills by interacting with customers constantly.
-Handled business transactions and was responsible for collecting certain amount of money by the end of the night.

5/07-7/07   **Kids Summer Camp**   Other Town, Different State
Counselor
-Responsible for watching and caring for kids of different ages
-Communicated with kids and parents and reassured them of their children's safety under my supervision.
-Coordinated and taught science and computer classes for children between ages of 6 to 16.

9/06-5/06   **Local Italian Food Restaurant**   New Town,
State

Server/Host
-Handled incoming calls with customers and fellow employees.
-Organized seating charts and sat customers and handled to go orders.
-Responsible for collecting and balancing transactions on all tickets at the end of the shifts.

ACTIVITIES: Society of Engineering Club   New Town, State
-Member for two years and Treasurer Sophomore year
CIS Local Association for Students   New Town, State
Hiking, rock climbing, outdoor sports

SKILLS: Proficient with the Internet, Microsoft Word, Excel, Access, all forms of Windows
Trained in all engineering based software program for use in office settings
Excellent computer and critical thinking skills from jobs and school
Outstanding customer service skills from jobs

References available upon request

Andrew Frankin

Afrankin@email.university.edu
(555) 555-1212

Current Address:	Permanent Address:
555 North Central Avenue Apt. #2	111 South 4th Street
New Town, State 80000	Old Town, Other State 50000

Objective: To secure a career opportunity with XYZ Company as a Level 1 Engineer to use my technical, analytical, and communication skills for improved productivity.

Education: **University of State** New Town, State December 2012
Bachelor of Science
Major: Engineering
Minor: Computer Sciences

Work Experience:
Anderson Engineering Firm Old Town, Other State May 2009 - July 2009
Intern
- Developed tracking format in Excel for monitoring customer contact and ongoing projects.
- Contacted external customers (eg; local utilities and construction companies) for partnering opportunities.
- Communicated project logistics to external customers for follow up from management team meetings.
- Transported confidential client documentation to project sites and customer offices.

Hometown Restaurant New Town, State May 2008 - August 2008
Server
- Increased revenue through promotion of additional appetizer and dessert items to fifty customers nightly.
- Maintained positive dining environment with team of 4 servers and bussers for twenty table restaurant.
- Collaborated with management on catering orders to off-site venues with 100% customer satisfaction.

Kids' Summer Camp Old Town, Other State May 2007 – August 2007
Counselor
- Created science and computer activities involving thirty children from multiple age groups.
- Developed construction and engineering-based activities for children age 6-10 to encourage teamwork.
- Communicated directly with parents regarding camp objectives and children's concerns.

Organizations:
Society of Engineering Club New Town, State August 2008 - Present
Treasurer August 2009 – Present
- Manage budget of $5000 for student organization with 28 members with a focus in engineering sciences.

CIS Local Association for Students New Town, State August 2009 - Present
- Utilize engineering concepts to compete in regional and national project symposiums annually.
- Coordinate weekly meetings with a team of five students to meet deadlines and project goals.

Big Bro Big Sis Program New Town, State December 2007 – Present
- Participate in bi-monthly academic and recreational activities with an underprivileged student.

Computer Skills:
- Microsoft Word, Excel, Outlook, Access
- Specialized engineering systems including ABC Program, Cision, and Exipro 3.5

Extra Resources:

Career Services/Career Center Departments

- Depending on the college or university, you may have access to career counselors who can help take a look at your resume after you create it.

www.bestresumebuilder.com

- If you want to use a program which will walk you through, step by step, in less than a half hour, check out this resource. Created specifically for collegiates and recent grads, it's specific and easy to use.

Other resume books

- If your specialty has different special circumstances, you can look for resume books tailored to your specialty. Just be careful not to over-complicate your resume for the reader!

INDEX

	Page
Address	3
Bullet points	13–14, 16
Certifications	22
Checklist	30–31
Clubs	18–20
Computer skills	24–25
Contact information	2–4
Education	9–11
Email address	4
GPA	10
Greek Life	19–20
High school information	9–10
Internships	13
Job experience	13–15
Language skills	27–28
Licenses	22
Majors	9
Minors	9
Name	2
Objective	6–7
Organization experience	18–20
Overseas Study	11
Phone number	2
References	31
Sample resumes	32–39
School information	9–11
Skills	14
SMART	14
Sports organizations	10, 16
Summary of skills	6–7
Technological skills	24–25
Traits	6
Volunteer experience	18–20
Work experience	13–15

I think

Coming Soon in the (I think) ™

Career Skills Series:

ACKNOWLEDGEMENTS

To the college students I have had the privilege of working with over the past two decades that are now in positions throughout corporate America, thank you for helping me understand what works and what doesn't.

To Sarah, thank you for the support and questions throughout the past year. For my colleagues in recruiting who have read thousands of resumes annually, thank you for looking at a few more for me and giving your valuable perspective.

To Mark for his support during this process and for watching over it now and forever.

To Tyler – you continue to be the ultimate inspiration, even though you may not know it.

ABOUT THE AUTHOR

Stacie Garlieb is the President of Successful Impressions, LLC. which assists collegiates and recent graduates with career search processes and skills. She has been featured several times on NBC television and KFYI radio during morning and evening news with interview tips. In partnership with University of Phoenix, Stacie is the creator and presenter for the 'Career Workshop Series' on resume building, interview preparation, interview skills, social media networking, and 're-careering' and transition in the workforce.

Stacie has been a seminar speaker for 'Build Your Career Event' (Career Builder/University of Phoenix) and the Arizona Women's Expo. Her career search tips and interview skills advice have been published in national sorority and university alumni publications. Through group presentations and one-on-one coaching on all career search related topics, she has worked with public and private college students nationally since 1991. In collaboration with businesses in various fields, she actively develops internship programs and recruits at public and private universities as well as career fairs.

Stacie was invited by California State Sacramento and University of the Pacific to act as a Career Consultant to the career services departments. She developed the Career Fair Training Program for University of the Pacific, and assisted in writing the "Career Services Interview Skills" guide. Over more than twenty years, she has worked for Fortune 500 organizations in sales, marketing, and management positions with recruiting responsibility after earning her Bachelor of Science from Arizona State University.

If you would like to know more about Stacie Garlieb's company or her seminars please visit her website at www.successfulimpressions.net

WILLIAM WOODS UNIVERSITY

7023392R0

Made in the USA
Lexington, KY
13 October 2010